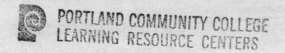
PORTLAND COMMUNITY COLLEGE
LEARNING RESOURCE CENTERS

DOVER · THRIFT · EDITIONS

Selected Poems
from
"Flowers of Evil"

CHARLES BAUDELAIRE

Selected and Translated by
Wallace Fowlie

D1025740

DOVER PUBLICATIONS, INC.
New York

DOVER THRIFT EDITIONS

GENERAL EDITOR: STANLEY APPELBAUM
EDITOR OF THIS VOLUME: THOMAS CROFTS

Copyright

Copyright © 1963, 1964 by Bantam Books, Inc.
Copyright © renewed 1991, 1992 by Wallace Fowlie.
All rights reserved under Pan American and International Copyright
Conventions.

Published in Canada by General Publishing Company, Ltd., 30 Lesmill Road,
Don Mills, Toronto, Ontario.
Published in the United Kingdom by Constable and Company, Ltd., 3 The
Lanchesters, 162–164 Fulham Palace Road, London W6 9ER.

Bibliographical Note

This Dover edition, first published in 1995, contains the complete English text
of *Flowers of Evil*, in selection, as it appeared in *Flowers of Evil and Other Works/Les
Fleurs du Mal et Oeuvres Choisies: A Dual-Language Book*, Dover Publications, Inc.,
New York, 1992. Lists of Titles and First Lines, as well as an introductory Note,
have been prepared specially for the present edition. As well, a small number of
Professor Fowlie's explanatory notes have been carried over or adapted and
appear on page 50 of the present volume, which is published by special arrange-
ment with Professor Fowlie.

Library of Congress Cataloging-in-Publication Data

Baudelaire, Charles, 1821–1867.
  [Fleurs du mal. English. Selections]
  Selected poems from "Flowers of evil" / Charles Baudelaire ; translated by
Wallace Fowlie.
      p.   cm. — (Dover thrift editions)
  Includes index.
  ISBN 0-486-28450-6
  I. Fowlie, Wallace, 1908–   II. Title.   III. Series.
PQ2191.F62E5   1995
841'.8—dc20   94-42022
                                                                              CIP

Manufactured in the United States of America
Dover Publications, Inc., 31 East 2nd Street, Mineola, N.Y. 11501

Note

THE CONTRIBUTION OF CHARLES BAUDELAIRE (1821–1867), not only to French poetry but to modern poetry in general, would be difficult to exaggerate. One of the things he did was to bring poetry largely out of Romanticism, in which poets commonly erected fantastic structures in the air and wove elaborate fictional narratives. Not interested in classical pomp or personal histrionics, Baudelaire composed lucidly, and with unwavering frankness, from his own (albeit sometimes hallucinatory) observations. Among prostitutes, drug dens, the suffering poor, and various other examples of Paris' moral ruin, but also in animals and children, he discovered images of the soul. These he worked into poems of brooding, desire and, at times, moving praise for the beauty he believed existed beneath the perversity and corruption of modern civilization.

Flowers of Evil (*Les Fleurs du Mal*, 1857), the work in which Baudelaire's genius is perhaps most concentrated, is a collection of poems of the greatest formal beauty and profoundest melancholy. Though this work is the result of an intensely personal mission, the exploration of pain, the poet's goal is neither to express his own unhappiness, nor to demonstrate his technical mastery, but to tear down the screens behind which our inner lives are so easily hidden, to follow his demons with true abandon, and, equally, to respond to beauty whenever blessed with a glimpse of it. Nineteenth-century France did not know quite what to make of this approach, and, on the publication of *Les Fleurs du Mal*, the author was prosecuted for obscenity and blasphemy, fined and forced to remove certain pieces from the book (restored in the key 1861 edition).

As well as a poet, Baudelaire was an important art and literary critic, and an early champion and translator of Edgar Allan Poe.

Note: an asterisk indicates an explanatory note on page 50.

Contents

Selected Poems

from

"Flowers of Evil"

FLOWERS OF EVIL

TO THE READER

Folly, error, sin and avarice
Occupy our minds and waste our bodies,
And we feed our polite remorse
As beggars feed their lice.

Our sins are stubborn, our repentance is cowardly;
We ask high prices for our vows,
And we gaily return to the muddy road,
Believing we will wash away all our spots with vile tears.

On the pillow of evil it is Thrice-Great Satan
Who endlessly rocks our bewitched mind,
And the rich metal of our will
Is vaporized by that wise chemist.

It is the Devil who pulls the strings that move us!
In repulsive objects we find enticing lures;
Each day we go down one more step toward Hell,
Without horror, through the darkness which smells rank.

Just as a lustful pauper who kisses and bites
The martyred breast of an aged whore,
We steal, as we move along, a clandestine pleasure
Which we squeeze hard like an old orange.

Packed tight and swarming like a million maggots,
A crowd of Demons carouse in our brains,
And, when we breathe, Death into our lungs
Descends, an invisible river, with heavy wailings.

If rape, poison, the knife and arson
Have not yet woven with their pleasing patterns
The banal canvas of our pitiful fate,
It is because our soul, alas, is not bold enough.

But among the jackals, panthers, bitches,
Monkeys, scorpions, vultures, serpents,
The monsters squealing, yelling, grunting, crawling
In the infamous menagerie of our vices

There is one uglier, more wicked and more foul than all!
Although he does not make great gestures or great cries,
He would gladly make the earth a shambles
And swallow the world in a yawn;

It is boredom! his eyes weeping an involuntary tear,
He dreams of gibbets as he smokes his hookah.
You know him, reader, this delicate monster,
—Hypocrite reader—my twin—my brother!

THE BLESSING

When, by a decree of the sovereign powers,
The Poet comes into this bored world,
His mother, terrified and full of blasphemy,
Clenches her fists toward God, who has pity on her:

"Ah, why didn't I litter a nest of vipers,
Rather than give birth to this mockery?
A curse on that night with its fleeting pleasures
When my womb conceived my expiation!

Since you chose me from among all women
To be the disgust of my disappointed husband,
And since I cannot throw back into the fire
This weak monster, like a love letter,

I will make your hate which stifles me gush forth
On the accursed instrument of your plottings,
And I will twist this wretched tree so far
That its blighted buds will not grow!"

Thus she swallows the foam of her hate,
And, without understanding the eternal designs,
She prepares in the pit of Hell
The pyres consecrated to the crimes of a mother.

Meanwhile, under the invisible care of an Angel,
The disinherited Child is intoxicated with sunlight,

And in all he drinks and in all he eats
Discovers ambrosia and vermillion nectar.

He plays with the wind, talks with the cloud,
And singing revels in the way of the cross;
And the Spirit following him in his pilgrimage
Weeps at seeing him happy as a bird in the forest.

All those he would love look at him with fear,
Or, emboldened by his calm manner,
Vie with one another in drawing from him a complaint
And practice on him the experiments of their cruelty.

In the bread and wine destined for his mouth
They mingle ashes with filthy spittings;
Hypocritically they throw away what he touches,
And blame themselves for stepping where he stepped.

His wife cries in the public places:
"Since he finds me beautiful enough to worship,
I will take on the profession of ancient idols,
And like them I will cover my body with gold;

And I will get drunk on nard, incense, myrrh,
Genuflections, meats and wines,
To learn if I can from an admiring heart
Laughingly usurp the homage of the gods!

And, when I am bored with these impious farces,
I will lay on him my frail and strong hand;
And my nails, like the nails of harpies,
Will dig a path to his heart.

Like a very young bird trembling and palpitating
I will pull that red heart out from his breast,
And, in order to satiate my favorite beast,
Scornfully I will throw it to him on the ground!"

Toward Heaven, where his eyes see a shining throne,
The serene Poet raises his reverent arms,
And the vast visions of his lucid mind
Shut off from him the sight of cruel races:

"Be blessed, my Lord, who give suffering
As a divine remedy for our impurities

And as the best and the purest essence
Which prepares the strong for holy ecstasies!

I know that you keep a place for the Poet
In the blessed ranks of the holy legions,
And that you invite him to the eternal feast
Of Thrones, Virtues and Dominations.

I know that suffering is the one nobility
Where the earth and hell will have no effect,
And that in order to weave my mystic crown
All times and all worlds must be used.

But the lost jewels of ancient Palmyra,
The unknown metals, the pearls of the sea,
Mounted by your hand, could not suffice
For this handsome diadem shining and clear;

For it will be made only of pure light,
Drawn from the holy hearth of primal rays,
And to which mortal eyes, in their full splendor,
Are but tarnished and sad mirrors!"

THE ALBATROSS

Often, as an amusement, crewmen
Catch albatrosses, huge birds of the sea,
Who follow, indolent companions of the voyage,
The ship gliding over the salty deeps.

As soon as they have placed them on the deck,
These kings of the sky, awkward and ashamed,
Pitiably let their large white wings
Drag at their sides like oars.

This winged voyager, how gauche and weak he is!
Once so handsome, how comic and ugly he is!
One sailor irritates his beak with a pipestem,
Another mimes, as he limps, the invalid who once flew!

The Poet is like the prince of the clouds,
Who haunts the tempest and mocks the archer;
Exiled on the earth in the midst of derision,
His giant wings keep him from walking.

ELEVATION

Above ponds, above valleys,
Mountains, woods, clouds, seas,
Beyond the sun, beyond the ether,
Beyond the limits of the starry spheres,

My spirit, you move with agility,
And, like a good swimmer who collapses in the water,
You gaily furrow the deep expanse
With an unspeakable male delight.

Fly far away from these fetid marshes;
Purify yourself in the upper air,
And drink, like some pure divine liqueur,
The clear fire that fills the limpid spaces.

Behind the boredom and endless cares
Which burden our fogged existence with their weight,
Happy is the man who can with vigorous wing
Mount to those luminous serene fields!

The man whose thoughts, like larks,
Take liberated flight toward the morning skies
—Who hovers over life and understands without effort
The language of flowers and voiceless things!

CORRESPONDENCES

Nature is a temple where living pillars
At times allow confused words to come forth;
There man passes through forests of symbols
Which observe him with familiar eyes.

Like long echoes which in a distance are mingled
In a dark and profound unison
Vast as night is and light,
Perfumes, colors and sounds answer one another.

There are perfumes as cool as the flesh of children,
Sweet as oboes, green as prairies
—And others, corrupt, rich and triumphant,

Having the expansion of infinite things,
Like amber, musk, myrrh and incense,
Which sing of the transports of the mind and the senses.

BEACONS

Rubens, river of forgetfulness, garden of idleness,
Pillow of cool flesh where one cannot love,
But where life abounds and writhes ceaselessly,
Like air in the sky and the sea in the sea;

Leonardo da Vinci, deep and dark mirror,
Where charming angels, with a sweet smile
Charged with mystery, appear under the shadow
Of glaciers and pines which shut in their country;

Rembrandt, sad hospital filled with murmurings,
And decorated only with a large crucifix,
Where tearful prayers are exhaled from excrement
And abruptly crossed by a winter ray;

Michelangelo, vague place where are seen Hercules
Mingling with Christs, and rising upright
Powerful phantoms which at twilight
Rip open their shrouds when they stretch their fingers;

Anger of the wrestler, impudence of the faun,
You who collected the beauty of soldiers,
Noble heart swollen with pride, weak jaundiced man,
Puget, melancholy emperor of convicts;

Watteau, that carnival where many illustrious hearts,
Like moths, wander as flames catch them,
Fresh, light decors illuminated by chandeliers
Which pour madness over the turning dance;

Goya, nightmare filled with unknown things,
With foetuses which are cooked in the midst of a witch's
    feast,
Of old women at a mirror and naked girls
Adjusting their stockings to tempt the demons;

Delacroix, lake of blood haunted by evil angels,
Under the shadow of a green forest of firs,

Where, under a gloomy sky, strange fanfares
Pass, like a muffled sigh of Weber;

These curses, blasphemies, complaints,
These ecstasies, cries, tears, these *Te Deums*,
Are an echo repeated by a thousand labyrinths;
They are for the hearts of men a divine opium!

It is a cry repeated by a thousand sentinels,
An order returned by a thousand loud-speakers;
It is a beacon lighted on a thousand citadels,
A call of hunters lost in the deep woods!

For it is in truth, O Lord, the best testimonial
We can give of our dignity—
This ardent sobbing which rolls from age to age
And comes to die at the edge of your eternity!

THE ENEMY

My youth was a dark storm,
Crossed here and there by brilliant suns;
Thunder and rain have caused such quick ravage
That there remain in my garden very few red fruits.

Now I have touched the autumn of my mind,
And I must use the spade and rakes
To assemble again the drenched lands,
Where the water digs holes as large as graves.

And who knows whether the new flowers I dream of
Will find in this soil washed like a shore
The mystic food which would create their strength?

—O grief! O grief! Time eats away life,
And the dark Enemy who gnaws the heart
Grows and thrives on the blood we lose.

ILL LUCK

To raise a weight so heavy,
Sisyphus, we would need your courage!
Although we have a strong heart for the work,
Art is long and Time is short.

Far from famous graves,
Toward a lonely cemetery,
My heart, like a muffled drum,
Comes beating a funeral march.

—Many a gem lies buried
In darkness and oblivion,
Far from pickaxes and drills;

Many a flower pours forth regretfully
Its perfume sweet as a secret
In solitary shades.

FORMER LIFE

A long time I lived under vast porticoes
Which marine suns tinged with a thousand fires,
And which their tall pillars, straight and majestic,
Caused to resemble basalt caves at night.

The surge, as it rolled images of the sky,
Mingled in a solemn mystical way
The omnipotent harmonies of its rich music
With the colors of the setting sun reflected in my eyes.

It is there I lived in serene sensuousness,
In the midst of blue sky, waves, splendor
And naked slaves, impregnated with perfumes,

Who cooled my brow with palms,
And whose one care was to understand
The grievous secret which made me sad.

MAN AND THE SEA

Free man, you will always cherish the sea!
The sea is your mirror; you contemplate your soul
In the infinite rolling of its surface,
And your spirit is not a less bitter abyss.

You take pleasure in plunging into the heart of your
        image;
You embrace it with your eyes and your arms, and your
        heart

At times forgets its own rhythm
In the noise of that wild and tameless complaint.

Both of you are dark and discreet:
Man, no one has sounded the depths of your being,
Sea, no one knows your intimate secrets,
So eager are you to retain your secrets!

And yet for countless centuries
You have fought without pity and without remorse,
So much do you love carnage and death,
O eternal fighters, O implacable brothers!

DON JUAN IN HELL

When Don Juan descended to the lower water
And when he had given his fee to Charon,
A solemn beggar, with eyes as proud as Antisthenes,
Seized each oar with an avenging strong arm.

Showing their drooping breasts and their opened dresses,
Some women were swaying under the black firmament,
And, like a large herd of sacrificed victims,
Trailed behind him with long moans.

Sganarelle laughing asked him for his wages,
While Don Luis with a trembling finger
Pointed out to all the dead wandering on the banks
The bold son who mocked his white brow.

Trembling under her veils, chaste and thin Elvira,
Near the perfidious husband who had been her lover,
Seemed to claim from him one last smile
Where the sweetness of his first vows would shine forth.

Upright in his armor, a tall man of stone
Stood at the helm and cleft the dark waves;
But the calm hero, leaning on his sword,
Looked at the wake and did not deign to see anything
    else.

BEAUTY

I am as beautiful, O mortals! as a dream of stone,
And my breast, on which each man is wounded in turn,
Is made to inspire in the poet a love
As eternal and mute as matter.

I preside in the heavens like a misunderstood sphinx;
I unite a heart of snow with the whiteness of swans;
I hate all movement which displaces lines,
And I never weep and I never laugh.

The poets before my great poses,
Which I seem to borrow from the proudest monuments,
Will consume their days in austere studies;

For I have, in order to fascinate these docile lovers,
Pure mirrors which make all things more beautiful:
My eyes, my large eyes with their eternal light!

THE GIANTESS

At that time when Nature in her powerful ardor
Conceived monstrous children each day,
I would have loved living near a young giantess,
As a voluptuous cat at the feet of a queen.

I should like to have seen her body flower with her soul
And grow freely in her dreadful games;
And guess whether her heart conceals a somber flame
From the wet fog swimming in her eyes;

Feel at my leisure her magnificent shape;
Climb on the slope of her huge knees,
And at times in summer, when the unhealthy suns,

Wearying, make her stretch out across the country,
Sleep without worry in the shade of her breast,
Like a peaceful hamlet at the foot of a mountain.

THE MASK

An allegorical statue
in the style of the Renaissance

To Ernest Christophe, sculptor

Let us look at this treasure of Florentine grace;
In the curves of this muscular body
Elegance and Force abound, divine sisters.
This woman, a truly miraculous work,
Divinely strong, adorably thin,
Is made to preside over sumptuous beds,
And charm the idleness of a pontiff or of a prince.

—Also, see that enticing voluptuous smile
In which Fatuity parades its ecstasy;
That long sly look, languorous and mocking;
That charming face, surrounded by a veil,
In which each feature tells us with a triumphant air:
"Passion calls me and Love crowns me!"
To that being endowed with such majesty
See what exciting charm kindness gives!
Let us approach, and walk around her beauty.

Oh blasphemy of art! Oh fatal shock!
The woman with the divine body, promising happiness,
Ends at the top in a two-headed monster!

—No! this face is only a mask, a wicked ornament,
Illuminated by an exquisite grimace,
Look and see, atrociously contorted,
The real head, and the sincere face
Turned back under the shadow of the face which lies.
Poor noble beauty! the magnificent river
Of your tears ends in my anxious heart;
Your lie intoxicates me, and my soul drinks
From the waves which Grief causes to gush from your
    eyes!

—But why does she cry? She, a perfected beauty
Who would cast at her feet mankind conquered,
What mysterious malady eats into her supple side?

PORTLAND COMMUNITY COLLEGE
LEARNING RESOURCE CENTER

—O fool, she cries because she has lived!
And because she is living! But what she deplores
Above all, what makes her tremble to her knees,
Is that tomorrow, alas! she will have to live again!
Tomorrow, the day after tomorrow and forever—as we
    have to!

HYMN TO BEAUTY

Do you come from deep heaven or do you come from
    hell,
O Beauty? Your eyes, infernal and divine,
Pour out both goodness and crime,
And for that you can be compared to wine.

You contain in your eyes the sunset and dawn;
You scatter perfumes like a stormy night;
Your kisses are a philtre and your mouth an amphora
Which make the hero a coward and the child courageous.

Do you come from a black abyss or do you come down
    from the stars?
Charmed Destiny follows your skirts like a dog;
At random you sow joy and disasters,
And you govern all and answer for nothing.

You walk over the dead, O Beauty, and mock them.
Among your jewels, Horror is not the least charming,
And Murder, among your dearest baubles,
Dances amorously on your proud body.

The dazzled moth flies to you, a candle,
Crackles, flames and says: Let us bless this torch!
The panting lover bending over his mistress
Resembles a dying man caressing his tomb.

It is of little consequence whether you come from heaven
    or hell,
O Beauty! huge, terrifying, artless monster!
If your eyes, your smile, your feet open for me the gate
Of an Infinity I love and have never known.

From Satan or God, what difference? Angel or Siren,
What difference, if you make—O fairy with soft eyes,
Rhythm, perfume, light, O my one queen—
The universe less hideous and time less heavy?

HER HAIR

O fleece, which covers her neck like wool!
O curls! O perfume heavy with nonchalance!
Ecstasy! Tonight, in order to people this dark alcove
With the memories sleeping in this hair,
I want to shake it in the air like a handkerchief!

Languorous Asia and burning Africa,
A whole distant world, absent, almost defunct,
Lives in your depths, O aromatic forest!
As other spirits sail on music,
Mine, O my love, swims on your perfume.

I will go there where the tree and man, full of sap,
Swoon for a long time under the ardor of the climate;
Strong tresses, be the ocean swell which carries me off!
You contain, O sea of ebony, a dazzling dream
Of sails and rowers of flames and masts:

A resounding port where my soul can drink
In long draughts perfume, sound and color;
Where ships, gliding in the gold and mixed shades,
Open their vast arms to embrace the glory
Of a pure sky where eternal heat quivers.

I shall plunge my head in love with intoxication
Into that black ocean where she is enclosed;
And my subtle spirit which the rolling surface caresses
Will be able to find you again, O fertile idleness!
Infinite rockings of my embalmed leisure!

Blue hair, tent of stretched darkness,
You give me back the blue of the huge round sky;
On the downy edges of your twisted locks
My ardor grows drunk on the mingled smells
Of coconut oil, of musk and tar.

For a long time! forever! my hand in your heavy mane
Will sow rubies, pearls and sapphires,
So that you will never be deaf to my desire!
Are you not the oasis where I dream, and the gourd
From which I draw in long draughts the wine of mem-
ory?

"I WORSHIP YOU"

I worship you as I worship the firmament of night,
O urn of sadness, great silent woman,
And love you, beautiful one, the more you flee from me,
And seem to me, ornament of my nights,
To accumulate ironically the leagues
Which separate my arms from the expanse of blue.

I advance to the attack, and I climb to the assault,
As a chorus of worms climb over a corpse,
And I cherish, O implacable cruel beast,
Even that coldness by which you are for me more beau-
tiful!

A CARRION

Remember the object we saw, dear one,
    On that fine summer morning so mild:
At the turn of a path a loathsome carrion
    On a bed sown with pebbles,

Its legs in the air, like a lubricious woman,
    Burning and sweating venom,
Opened in a nonchalant cynical way
    Her body full of stench.

The sun shone on that rottenness,
    As if to roast it thoroughly,
And return a hundredfold to great Nature
    All that it joined together.

And the sky looked at the superb carcass
    Like a flower blossoming.
The smell was so strong that there on the grass
    You believed you might faint.

The flies swarmed over the putrid belly,
From which emerged black battalions
Of maggots, which flowed like a thick liquid
Along those human rags.

All of it descended, or rose like a wave,
Or rushed forth buzzing;
One might have said that the body, swollen with a
vague breath,
Lived by multiplying itself.

And that world gave forth a strange music,
Like running water and wind,
Or the grain which a winnower in rhythmic motion
Shakes and turns in his basket.

The shapes had dimmed and were only a dream,
A sketch slow to emerge
On the forgotten canvas, and which the artist finishes
Only by memory.

Behind rocks a restless bitch
Watched us with an angry eye,
Waiting for the moment to take from the skeleton
The piece it had relinquished.

—And yet you will be similar to that filth,
To that horrible infection,
Star of my eyes, sun of my nature,
You, my angel and my passion!

Yes! you will be like that, O queen of graces,
After the last sacraments,
When you go, under the grass and rich blossomings,
To rot among the bones.

Then, O my beauty, tell the vermin
Which will eat you with kisses,
That I have kept the form and the divine essence
Of my decomposed loves!

DE PROFUNDIS CLAMAVI *

I implore your pity, You, the only one I love,
From the depth of the dark abyss where my heart fell.
It is a mournful universe with a leaden horizon,
Where horror and blasphemy swim in the night;

A sun without heat hovers above for six months,
And the other six months night covers the earth;
It is a country more bare than the polar land
—No beasts, no streams, no green, no woods!

For there is no horror in the world which surpasses
The cold cruelty of that icy sun
And that vast night similar to the old Chaos;

I envy the fate of the lowest animals
Who can sink into a stupid sleep,
Because the skein of time is so slow to unravel!

DUELLUM *

Two warriors rushed at one another; their weapons
Splashed the air with streaks of light and blood.
These plays, this clinking of steel are the tumult
Of youth prey to bleating love.

The swords were broken! like our youth,
Beloved! But the teeth, the sharp nails,
Soon avenge the saber and the treacherous dagger
—O fury of matured hearts exasperated by love!

Into the ravine haunted by lynxes and leopards
Our heroes, wickedly wrestling, rolled,
And their skin will cover the arid briars with flowers.

—This abyss is hell, peopled with our friends!
Let us roll there without remorse, inhuman Amazon,
In order to make eternal the ardor of our hate!

THE BALCONY

Mother of memories, mistress of mistresses,
You, all my pleasures! You, all my duties!
You will remember the beauty of caresses,
The sweetness of the hearth and the spell of evenings,
Mother of memories, mistress of mistresses!

Evenings lighted by the burning of the coals,
And evenings on the balcony, veiled with rosy vapors.
How soft your breast was for me! how kind your heart
    was!
We often said imperishable things
On evenings lighted by the burning of the coals.

How beautiful the sun is in the warm evening!
How deep is space! How powerful is the heart!
As I bent over you, queen of worshiped women,
I believed I could smell the perfume of your blood.
How beautiful the sun is in the warm evening!

Night thickened as if it were a partition,
And my eyes in the dark could hardly see your eyeballs,
And I drank your breath, O sweetness, O poison!
And your feet went to sleep in my fraternal hands.
Night thickened as if it were a partition.

I know the art of evoking minutes of happiness,
And I saw again my past hidden in your knees.
Why look for your languorous beauty
Elsewhere than in your dear body and in your gentle
    heart?
I know the art of evoking minutes of happiness.

Will these vows, perfumes and infinite kisses
Be born again from an abyss forbidden to our soundings,
As rejuvenated suns climb in the heavens
After being washed at the bottom of deep seas?
—O vows! O perfumes! O infinite kisses!

"I GIVE YOU THESE VERSES"

I give you these verses so that if my name
Happily lands in distant epochs,
And one evening makes the human spirit dream,
Vessel favored by a great northwind,

The memory of you, resembling obscure fables,
Will weary the reader like a dulcimer,
And through a brotherly and mystic link
Remain as if hanging from my lofty rhymes;

Accursed one to whom, from the deep abyss
To the highest sky, nothing gives answer, save me!
You who like a shade with tracks ephemeral,

Walk with light step and serene glance
Over the stupid mortals who have judged you badly,
Statue with eyes of jet, great angel with your brow of
    brass!

SEMPER EADEM *

You used to say, "Whence comes to you this strange
    sadness,
Mounting like the sea over the black bare rock?"
When our heart has once made its vintage,
To live is a curse. It is a secret known to all,

A very simple grief and not mysterious,
And, like your joy, clear to everyone.
So stop your search, O beauty so curious,
And, even if your voice is sweet, be silent!

Be silent, you who are ignorant, whose soul is always
    charmed,
Whose lips have a child's laugh! Much more than Life,
Death often holds us by subtle bonds.

Let, yes, let my heart grow passionate on a *lie*,
Let it sink into your lovely eyes as into a lovely dream,
And sleep for a long time under the shadow of your
    lashes!

"WHAT WILL YOU SAY?"

What will you say this evening, poor solitary soul,
What will you say, my heart, heart once disgraced,
To that beauty who is kind and dear,
And whose divine glance has suddenly given you new
    life?

—We will place our pride in singing her praises:
Nothing is worth the sweetness of her authority;
The flesh of her spirit has the perfume of Angels,
And her eyes clothe us with a cloak of light.

Whether it be at night and in solitude,
Whether it be in the street and within a multitude,
Her phantom dances in the air like a torch.

Sometimes it speaks and says: "I am beautiful, and I
    command
That for my love you love only what is Beauty;
I am the guardian Angel, the Muse and the Madonna!"

DAWN OF THE SPIRIT

When with revelers the white crimson dawn
Comes to join the persistent Ideal,
Through the operation of an avenging mystery
An angel is awakened in the sated brute.

The inaccessible blue of Spiritual Skies,
For the crushed man who still dreams and suffers,
Opens and sinks down with the attraction of the abyss.
Thus, dear Goddess, lucid pure Being,

Over the smoky wrecks of stupid orgies
Your memory more clear, roseate, and charming,
Ceaselessly hovers before my wide-opened eyes.

The sun has darkened the flame of the candles;
Thus, always conquering, your phantom is like
The immortal sun, O soul of splendor!

EVENING HARMONY

Now comes the time when quivering on its stem
Each flower exhales like a censer;
Sounds and perfumes turn in the evening air;
Melancholy waltz and languorous vertigo!

Each flower exhales like a censer;
The violin sobs like an afflicted heart;
Melancholy waltz and languorous vertigo!
The sky is as sad and beautiful as a great altar of rest.

The violin sobs like an afflicted heart,
A tender heart, which hates the huge black void!
The sky is as sad and beautiful as a great altar of rest.
The sun drowned in its blood which coagulates.

A tender heart, which hates the huge black void,
Welcomes every vestige of a luminous past!
The sun drowned in its blood which coagulates . . .
Your memory shines in me like a monstrance!

AN INVITATION TO VOYAGE

My child, my sister,
Think of the delight
Of going far off and living together!
Of loving peacefully,
Loving and dying
In the land that bears your resemblance!
The wet suns
Of those disheveled skies
Have for my spirit
The mysterious charm
Of your treacherous eyes
Shining through their tears.

There, all is order and beauty,
Richness, quiet and pleasure.

Highly polished furniture,
Made beautiful by time,
Would decorate our room;

The rarest flowers
Mingling their odors
With the vague fragrance of amber,
Rich ceilings,
Deep mirrors,
Eastern splendor,
Everything there would speak
In secret to the soul
Its sweet native tongue.

There, all is order and beauty,
Richness, quiet and pleasure.

Behold sleeping
On the canals those ships
Whose temperament is a wanderer's;
It is to satisfy
Your slightest desire
That they come from the ends of the world.
—The setting sun
Clothes the fields,
The canals, the entire city,
With hyacinth and gold;
The world goes to sleep
In a warm light.

There, all is order and beauty,
Richness, quiet and pleasure.

IRREPARABLE

Can we stifle the old, the long Remorse,
Which lives, writhes and twists,
And feeds on us as the worm feeds on the dead,
As the maggot on the oak?
Can we stifle the implacable Remorse?

In what flask, in what wine, in what infusion,
Shall we drown this old enemy,
Destructive and ravenous as a courtesan,
Patient as an ant?
In what flask? in what wine? in what infusion?

Tell it, beautiful sorceress, yes, tell it, if you can,
        To this soul distraught with anguish
And like unto the dying man crushed by the wounded,
        And who is bruised by the horse's hoof.
Tell it, beautiful sorceress, yes, tell it, if you can,

To this dying man whom the wolf already detects
        And over whom the vulture is flying,
To this broken soldier! if he must despair
        Of having his cross and his tomb;
This poor dying man whom the wolf already detects!

Can one light up a murky black sky?
        Can one pierce darkness
Thicker than pitch, without morning and evening,
        Without stars, without funereal flashes?
Can one light up a murky black sky?

Hope which shines in the windows of the Inn
        Is blown out, and dead forever!
Without moon and rays, one can find where the martyrs
        Of a bad road are sheltered!
The Devil has made everything dark in the windows of
        the Inn!

Adorable sorceress, do you love the damned?
        Tell me, do you know what is irremissible?
Do you know Remorse, with the poisoned arrows,
        For which our heart serves as target?
Adorable sorceress, do you love the damned?

The Irreparable gnaws with its vile teeth
        Our soul, that pitiful monument,
And often it attacks, like the termite,
        The building at the foundation.
The Irreparable gnaws with its vile teeth!

—I have seen at times, upstage in a shoddy theater
        Which a resonant orchestra enflamed,
A fairy light up in an infernal sky
        A miraculous dawn;
I have seen at times upstage in a shoddy theater

A spirit, who was only light, gold and gauze,
     Fling to earth an enormous Satan;
But my heart, which ecstasy never visits,
     Is a theater where I wait,
Always in vain, for that Spirit with wings of gauze!

SONG OF AUTUMN

I

Soon we shall plunge into cold darkness;
Farewell, strong light of our too brief summers!
I already hear falling, with funereal thuds,
The wood resounding on the pavement of the court-
    yards.

All of winter will gather in my being: anger,
Hate, chills, horror, hard and forced labor,
And, like the sun in its polar hell,
My heart will be only a red icy block.

I listen shuddering to each log that falls;
The scaffold which is being built has not a hollower
    echo.
My mind is like the tower which falls
Under the blows of the indefatigable heavy battering
    ram.

It seems to me, lulled by the monotonous thuds,
That somewhere a casket is being nailed in great haste.
For whom? Yesterday it was summer; here is autumn!
This mysterious noise sounds like a departure.

II

I love the green light of your long eyes,
Sweet beauty, but everything today is bitter for me,
And nothing, neither your love, nor the boudoir, nor
    the hearth,
Is worth as much to me as the sun shining over the sea.

But despite all that, love me, tender heart! be maternal,
Even for an ingrate, even for a wicked man;

Lover or sister, be the passing tenderness
Of a glorious autumn or of a setting sun.

A brief task! The grave is waiting; it is avid!
My head resting on your knees, let me
Enjoy, as I grieve for the white torrid summer,
The yellow gentle ray of the earlier season!

MOESTA ET ERRABUNDA *

Tell me, Agatha, does your heart, at times, fly away,
Far from the black ocean of the sordid city,
Toward another ocean where splendor breaks forth,
As blue, clear, and deep as virginity?
Tell me, Agatha, does your heart at times fly away?

The sea, the mighty sea, consoles our labor!
What demon endowed the sea, the raucous singer
Whom the huge organ of howling winds accompanies,
With this sublime function of nurse?
The sea, the mighty sea, consoles our labor!

Take me away, O train! carry me off, O ship!
Far! far! Here the mud is made from our tears!
—Is it true that at times the sad heart of Agatha
Says: Far from remorse, and crimes, and grief,
Take me away, O train, carry me off, O ship?

How far away you are, perfumed paradise,
Where under a clear blue all is love and joy,
Where all that one loves is worthy of being loved,
Where in pure sensation the heart is drowned!
How far away you are, perfumed paradise!

But the green paradise of childish loves,
Races, songs, kisses, bouquets,
Violins vibrating behind the hills,
With jars of wine, at evening, in the groves
—But the green paradise of childish loves,

That innocent paradise, full of furtive joys,
Is it already farther away than India and China?

Can we remember with plaintive cries,
And still animate with a silver voice,
That innocent paradise full of furtive joys?

CATS

Fervent lovers and austere scholars
Both love, in their mature season,
The powerful gentle cats, pride of the house,
Which like them are sensitive to the cold and sedentary.

Friends of science and ecstasy,
They search for silence and the horror of darkness;
Erebus would have taken them for his funereal steeds,
If they could bend their pride to slavery.

While dreaming they take the noble attitudes
Of great Sphinxes stretched out in the heart of the
    desert,
Which seem to sleep in an endless revery;

Their fecund loins are full of magic sparks,
And specks of gold, like fine sand,
Add vague stars to their mystical eyeballs.

THE BROKEN BELL

It is bitter and sweet, during winter nights,
To listen, near the fire which crackles and smokes,
To the distant memories slowly rising
At the noise of chimes singing in the fog.

Happy is the bell with the vigorous throat
Which, despite its age, alert and strong,
Faithfully sends forth its religious cry,
Like an old soldier standing sentinel under the tent!

My soul is cracked, and when in its boredom
It wishes to fill the cold air of night with its songs,
It often comes about that its weakened voice

Resembles the thick rattle of a wounded man forgotten
On the edge of a lake of blood, under a great pile of the
    dead,
And who dies, without moving, after tremendous efforts.

SPLEEN

Pluvius, irritated with the entire city,
Pours from his urn in great waves a dismal cold
Over the pale inhabitants of the neighboring cemetery
And mortality over the foggy outskirts.

My cat on the stones looking for a litter
Ceaselessly moves its thin mangy body;
The soul of an old poet wanders along the rain spout
With the sad voice of a chilblained phantom.

The bell mourns, and the smoky log
Accompanies in falsetto the wheezing clock,
While in a pack of cards full of filthy odors,

The fatal bequest of an old dropsical woman,
The handsome knave of hearts and the queen of spades
Talk darkly about their dead love.

HEAUTONTIMOROUMENOS *

Like a butcher I will strike you
Without anger and without hate
As Moses struck the rock!
And from your eyelid I will cause,

In order to irrigate my Sahara,
The waters of suffering to gush forth.
My desire swollen with hope
Will float on your salty tears

Like a vessel moving out from shore,
And in my heart which they will intoxicate
Your dear sobs will resound
Like a drum beating the charge!

Am I not a false chord
In the divine symphony,
Thanks to the voracious Irony
Which shakes and bites me?

The raucous girl is in my voice!
This black poison is my blood!
I am the sinister mirror
In which the megara looks at herself!

I am the wound and the blade!
I am the slap and the cheek!
I am the limbs and the wheel,
The victim and the executioner!

I am the vampire of my own heart
—One of the deserted men
Condemned to eternal laughter,
And who can no longer smile!

THE IRREMEDIABLE

I

An Idea, a Form, a Being
Leaving the blue and falling
Into a murky leaden Styx
Where no· eye of Heaven penetrates;

An Angel, impudent traveler
Tempted by love of the deformed,
At the bottom of a huge nightmare
Floundering like a swimmer,

And struggling, O funereal anguish!
Against a gigantic whirlpool
Which sings like madmen
And pirouettes in the darkness;

A spellbound wretch
In his futile gropings,
In order to flee a serpent-filled place,
Looking for light and a key;

One damned descending without lamp,
On the edge of an abyss whose stench
Betrays the wet depths
Of endless stairways with no rail,

Where clammy monsters watch
Whose large phosphorous eyes
Create a night still blacker
And leave only themselves visible;

A ship caught at the pole,
As in a crystal trap,
Looking for the fatal aperture
Through which it fell into this jail

—Clear emblems, perfect picture
Of an irremediable fortune,
Which makes one think that the Devil
Always does well everything he does!

II

Somber clear dialogue
Of a heart which has become its own mirror!
Well of Truth, clear and black,
Where a pale star trembles,

An ironic, infernal beacon,
Torch of satanic grace,
A unique solace and glory,
—Consciousness in doing Evil!

THE SWAN

To Victor Hugo

I

Andromache, I think of you! This small river,
Poor sad mirror where once shone
The immense majesty of your widow's grief,
This deceptive Simoïs which grows with your tears,

Suddenly enriched my fertile memory,
As I crossed the newly built Carrousel.
Old Paris is no more (the form of a city
Changes more quickly, alas, than the heart of a man);

I see only in my mind that camp of booths,
The piles of rough-hewn capitals and shafts,
The grass, the heavy blocks turned green by the water
    of pools,
And, shining on the tiles, the crowded bric-à-brac.

There once a menagerie spread out;
There I saw, one morning, at the time when under a cold
Clear sky Labor awakens, when the road
Pushes a dark storm through the silent air,

A swan which had escaped from its cage,
And, with its webby feet rubbing the dry pavement,
Was dragging its white plumage over the level ground.
Near a stream without water the bird opening its beak

Nervously bathed its wings in the dust,
And said, its heart full of its beautiful native lake:
"Water, when will you rain down? When will you
    thunder, O lightning?"
I see that wretched bird, a strange and fatal myth,

Toward the sky at times, like the man of Ovid,
Toward the ironic and cruelly blue sky,
Stretching its avid head over its convulsed neck,
As if it were addressing reproaches to God!

II

Paris changes! But nothing in my sadness
Has moved! new palaces, scaffoldings, blocks,
Old suburbs, everything becomes an allegory for me,
And my dear memories are heavier than rocks.

In front of the Louvre an image vexes me:
I think of my great swan, with its mad gestures,
Like exiles, ridiculous and sublime,
And devoured by an unrelenting desire! And then of
    you,

Andromache, fallen from the arms of a great husband,
A degraded animal, in the hands of proud Pyrrhus,
Near an empty tomb bent over in ecstasy;
Widow of Hector, alas, and wife of Helenus!

I think of the Negress, thin and phthisical,
Walking in mud, and looking, with haggard eyes,
For the absent palm trees of proud Africa
Behind the huge wall of fog;

Of whoever has lost what can never
Be found again! Of those who collapse in tears
And suckle Grief as if she were a kind wolf!
Of sickly orphans drying like flowers!

As if in a forest where my mind is exiled
An old memory sounds as in a blast from a horn!
I think of sailors forgotten on an island,
Of prisoners, of conquered men! . . . And of many
    others!

"THE WARM-HEARTED SERVANT"

The warm-hearted servant of whom you were jealous,
And who is sleeping her sleep under humble grass,
Yes, we should take her some flowers.
The dead, the poor dead, know deep grief,
And when October, the stripper of old trees, blows
Its melancholy wind around their marble stone,
Certainly they must find the living ungrateful
In sleeping, as they do, warmly between their sheets,
While, racked by ominous dreams,
Without a bedmate, without intimate talk,
Old frozen skeletons worked over by worms,
They feel the winter snow dripping away
And the century melting, when no friends and no family
Replace the tattered wreathes hanging on the grill,

When the log whistles and sings, if in the evening
I saw her sitting calmly in the armchair,
If, in a blue cold night of December,
I found her huddled in a corner of my room,

Sedate, and coming from the depths of her eternal bed
To shield with her maternal eyes the child grown to
    man,
What could I answer that pious soul,
When I see tears falling from her empty eyelids?

PARISIAN DREAM

To Constantin Guys

I

Of that terrible landscape,
Such as no mortal ever saw,
This morning the image,
Vague and distant, still excites me.

Sleep is full of miracles!
By a strange caprice
I had banished from that spectacle
Irregular vegetation,

And, a painter proud of my talent,
I enjoyed in my picture
The intoxicating monotony
Of metal, marble and water.

Babel of stairways and arcades,
It was an endless palace,
Full of reservoirs and cascades
Falling into a dull or darkened gold;

And heavy cataracts,
Like crystal curtains,
Hung, in shimmering light,
On metal walls.

Not with trees, but with colonnades
The sleeping ponds were surrounded,
Where huge nymphs,
Like women, were mirrored.

Sheets of water spread out, blue,
Between rose and green quays,

Through millions of leagues,
Toward the ends of the universe;

They were unheard-of stones
And magic waves; they were
Huge dazzling glaciers
In all they reflected!

Carefree and taciturn,
Ganges Rivers, in the firmament,
Poured the treasure of their urns
Into diamond abysses.

Architect of my own fantasies,
I made pass, at will,
Under a tunnel of precious stones
A conquered ocean;

And everything, even the color black,
Seemed polished, clear, prismatic;
The liquid encased its glory
In the crystallized ray.

There was no star, no vestige
Of a sun, even at the horizon of the sky,
To illumine these prodigies,
Which shone with a personal fire!

And over these moving marvels
Hovered (a terrifying novelty!
Everything for the eye, nothing for the ear!)
A silence of eternity.

II

On opening again my eyes full of flame
I saw the horror of my garret,
And felt, as I turned inwardly,
The sharp prick of accursed worries;

The clock with the funereal tones
Struck noon brutally,
And the sky poured darkness
Over the sad lethargic world.

MORNING TWILIGHT

Reveille sounded in the courtyard of the barracks,
And the morning wind blew on the lanterns.

It was the hour when the swarm of guilty dreams
Twists dark-haired adolescents on their pillows;
When, like a bleeding eye which throbs and moves,
The lamp makes a red spot on the daylight;
When the soul, under the weight of a reluctant heavy
    body,
Imitates the struggle between the lamp and the daylight.
Like a face covered with tears which the wind dries,
The air is full of the shuddering of things which flee,
And man is tired of writing and woman of loving.

Houses here and there began to send up smoke.
Prostitutes, with white eyelids,
And opened mouths, slept their stupid sleep;
Impoverished women, dragging their thin old breasts,
Blew on their burning logs and blew on their fingers.
It was the hour when in the cold and stinginess
The pain of women in labor grows greater;
Like a sob interrupted by thick blood
The distant song of the cock ripped through the foggy
    air;
A sea of fogs bathed the buildings,
And the dying in the depths of the hospitals
Uttered their last rattle in uneven gasps.
The revelers went home, broken by their work.

Shivering dawn in a rose-and-green dress
Slowly advanced over the deserted Seine,
And dark Paris, rubbing his eyes,
Took hold of his tools, a hard-working old man.

DESTRUCTION

Ceaselessly beside me the Demon writhes;
He swarms around me like impalpable air;
I swallow him and feel him burning my lungs
And filling them with an everlasting guilty desire.

At times he takes, knowing my great love for Art,
The form of the most seductive of women,
And, under specious pretexts of depression,
Accustoms my lips to infamous love charms.

Thus, far from the sight of God, he leads me,
Panting and crushed by fatigue, into the midst
Of the plains of Boredom, extensive and deserted,

And throws before my eyes full of confusion
Soiled clothing, opened wounds,
And the bloody apparatus of Destruction.

A MARTYR

Drawing of an Unknown Master

In the midst of flasks, gilt fabrics
        And rich furniture,
Marbles, pictures, perfumed dresses,
        Dragging with sumptuous folds,

In a warm room where, as in a hothouse,
        The air is dangerous and fatal,
Where dying bouquets in their glass caskets
        Exhale their last sigh,

A headless corpse sends forth, like a river,
        On the slaked pillow
A red living blood, which the cloth soaks up
        With the avidity of a meadow.

Similar to the pale visions which the darkness engenders
        And which captivate our eyes,
The head, with the mass of its dark hair
        And its precious jewels,

On the night table, like a ranunculus,
        Rests; and, emptied of thoughts,
A glance vague and white as twilight,
        Escapes from the revulsed eyes.

On the bed, the naked torso displays without scruple
        In the completest abandonment

The secret splendor and the fatal beauty
        With which nature endowed it;

On the leg, a rose-colored stocking, decorated with gold
            clocks,
        Remains like a souvenir;
The garter, like a flaming secret eye,
        Darts a diamondlike glance.

The singular aspect of this solitude
        And of a large languorous portrait,
With eyes as provocative as its pose,
        Reveals a secretive love,

A guilty joy and strange orgies
        Full of infernal kisses,
Over which the swarm of bad angels rejoiced
        As they swarm in the folds of the curtains;

And yet, on seeing the elegant thinness
        Of the shoulder with its abrupt shape,
The hip a bit pointed and the frisky figure
        Like an irritated snake,

She is still quite young! Had her exasperated soul
        And her senses bitten by boredom
Half opened to the greedy pack
        Of errant lost desires?

Did the vindictive man you were not able, when alive,
        In spite of so much love, to satisfy,
Release over your inert and complacent flesh
        The immensity of his desire?

Answer, impure corpse! And through your stiff tresses,
        Raising you with a feverish arm,
Tell me, terrifying head, did he on your cold teeth
        Imprint the last farewell?

—Far from the mocking world, far from the impure
            crowd,
        Far from curious magistrates,
Sleep in peace, sleep in peace, strange creature,
        In your mysterious tomb;

Your lover is far away, and your immortal form
    Watches near him when he sleeps;
As much as you doubtless he will be faithful
    And constant until death.

A VOYAGE TO CYTHERA

My heart, like a bird, flew about joyously
And hovered in freedom around the riggings;
The ship rolled under a sky without clouds,
Like an angel intoxicated with a radiant sun.

What is this sad dark island? It is Cythera,
They tell us, a famous country in songs,
The banal Eldorado of all the playboys.
Look! After all, it's a poor land.

—Island of sweet secrets and celebrations of the heart!
The proud phantom of ancient Venus
Hovers above your seas like an aroma,
And fills the mind with love and languor.

Beautiful island with green myrtle, full of opened
    flowers,
Venerated forever by all nations,
Where the sigh of adoring hearts
Rolls like incense over a garden of roses

Or the eternal cooing of a turtledove!
—Cythera was but a land of the most wasted kind,
A rocky desert disturbed by bitter cries.
Yet I could half distinguish an unusual object!

It was not a temple with bosky shadows,
Where the young priestess, lover of flowers,
Walked, her body burning with secret fire,
And her dress half opening in the passing breeze;

But there as we grazed the coast close enough
To disturb the birds with our white sails,
We saw it was a three-forked gallows,
Standing out in black from the sky, like a cypress.

Ravenous birds perched on their prey
Were ferociously demolishing a ripe body that had been
    hanged,
Each one planting, like an instrument, its impure beak
In all the bleeding parts of the rotting flesh;

The eyes were two holes, and from the collapsed belly
The heavy intestines flowed over the thighs,
And its tormentors, gorged with hideous food,
Had totally castrated it with their sharp beaks.

Under its feet, a flock of jealous beasts,
With uplifted muzzles, were moving and prowling
    about;
A very large animal in the middle behaved
Like a leader surrounded by his aides.

Inhabitant of Cythera, child of so beautiful a sky,
In silence you bore these insults
As expiation for your infamous cults
And for the sins which deprived you of a tomb.

Ridiculous victim of the gallows, your grief is mine!
When I saw your floating limbs, I felt,
Mounting toward my mouth, like a vomiting
The long stream of bile of old grief;

Before you, poor wretch with so precious a memory,
I felt all the beaks and all the jaws
Of lancinating crows and black panthers
Who once dearly loved to tear my flesh.

—The sky was charming, the sea unclouded;
For me all would be henceforth black and bloody,
Alas! and I had, as in a thick shroud,
Buried my heart in this allegory.

In your island, O Venus, I found standing
Only a symbolic gallows from which my image was
    hanging . . .
—O Lord, give me the strength and the courage
To contemplate without disgust my heart and my body!

DEATH OF THE LOVERS

We shall have beds full of faint perfumes,
Divans as deep as tombs,
And strange flowers on shelves,
Opened for us under more beautiful skies.

Using their last warmth in emulation,
Our two hearts will be two vast torches,
Which will reflect their double lights
In our two spirits, those twin mirrors.

One evening, made of mystical rose and blue,
We will exchange one flash of light,
Like a long sob, laden with farewells;

And later an Angel, half opening the doors,
Will come, faithful and joyous, to reanimate
The tarnished mirrors and the dead flames.

DEATH OF THE ARTISTS

How many times must I shake my clown's bells
And kiss your low brow, sad caricature?
In order to strike the target, of mystical nature,
How many javelins must I lose, O quiver?

We will wear out our souls in subtle schemes,
And dismantle many a heavy armor,
Before contemplating the great Creature
Whose infernal desire fills us with sobs!

There are some who have never known their Idol,
And those banned sculptors branded with an affront,
Who as they walk beat their chests and their brows,

Have but one hope, strange and somber Capitol!
It is that Death, hovering like a new sun,
Will cause the flowers of their minds to bloom!

THE VOYAGE

To Maxime Du Camp

I

For the child, in love with maps and prints,
The universe is equal to his huge appetite.
Ah! how large the world is under the lamplight!
In the eyes of memory, how small the world is!

One morning we leave, our minds full of fire,
Our hearts heavy with anger and bitter desire,
And we go, following the rhythm of the wave,
Rocking our infinity on the finiteness of the sea:

Some, happy to escape from an infamous land;
Others, from the horror of their cradles, and a few,
Astrologists drowning in the eyes of a woman,
A tyrannical Circe with her dangerous perfumes.

In order not to be changed into beasts, they are en-
    raptured
With space and light and burning skies;
The ice which freezes them, the sun which bronzes them,
Slowly efface the mark of kisses.

But the real travelers are those only who leave
In order to leave; light hearts, similar to balloons,
They are never separated from their fate,
And, without knowing why, always say: let us go on!

Those whose desires have the form of clouds,
And who dream, as a recruit dreams of a cannon,
Of vast, changing, and unknown raptures,
And whose name the human spirit has never known!

II

We imitate, O horror, the top and the bowl
In their waltz and their leap; even in our sleep
Curiosity torments and rolls us,
As a cruel Angel whipping the sun.

Singular fortune where the goal is displaced,
And, being nowhere, can be anywhere!
Where Man, whose hope never wearies,
In order to find rest is always rushing like a fool!

Our soul is a three-master searching for its Icaria;
A voice resounds on the deck: "Open your eyes!"
A voice from the watch, ardent and mad, cries:
"Love . . . fame . . . happiness!" Hell! it is a reef!

Each island pointed out by the watchman
Is an Eldorado promised by Destiny;
The Imagination which calls up its orgy
Finds only a sandbar in the morning light.

O the poor lover of chimerical lands!
Shall we put into irons, and cast into the sea,
This drunken sailor, inventor of Americas
Whose mirage makes the deep more bitter?

As the old tramp, groveling in the mud,
Dreams, his nose in the air, of brilliant paradises;
His bewitched eyes discover a Capua
Wherever the candle lights up a hovel.

III

Amazing travelers! What noble histories
We read in your eyes as deep as the sea!
Show us the caskets of your rich memories,
The marvelous jewels, made of stars and rays.

We want to voyage without steam and without sail!
To enliven the boredom of our prisons,
Send over our minds, as taut as a canvas,
Your memories with their frames of horizons.

Tell me, what did you see?

IV

"We saw stars
And waves; we saw sand also;

And, despite many shocks and unforeseen disasters,
We were often bored, as here.

The glory of the sun on the violet sea,
The glory of the cities in the setting sun,
Lighted up in our hearts a restless yearning
To plunge into a sky with an alluring reflection.

The richest cities, the widest landscapes,
Never contained the mysterious attraction
Of those which chance creates with clouds.
And always desire made us worried!

—Satisfaction adds strength to desire.
Desire, old tree to which pleasure serves as manure,
While your bark grows and hardens,
Your branches want to see the sun at closer range!

Will you continue to grow, huge tree with longer life
Than the cypress?—But we have carefully
Picked a few sketches for your voracious album,
Brothers who find beautiful everything that comes from
    far off!

We have greeted idols with a trunk;
Thrones studded with luminous jewels;
Decorated palaces whose fantasylike pomp
Would be for your bankers a ruinous dream;

Costumes which are an intoxication for the eyes:
Women whose teeth and nails are tinted,
And learned jugglers caressed by a serpent."

v

And after that, what after that?

VI

                    "O childish minds!

In order not to forget the important thing,
We have seen everywhere, and without looking for it,
From the top to the bottom of the fatal ladder,
The boring spectacle of immortal sin:

Woman, a low slave, proud and stupid,
Worshiping herself without laughter and loving herself
    without disgust;
Man, a greedy tyrant, lustful, hard and envious,
Slave of the slave and rivulet in the sewer;

The executioner who has his pleasure, the martyr who
    sobs;
The festivity heightened and perfumed by blood;
The poison of power irritating the despot,
And the crowd in love with the crushing whip;

Several religions similar to ours,
All of them climbing to heaven; His Holiness,
As on a feather bed a refined man wallows,
In nails and horsehair looking for his pleasure;

Talkative Humanity, intoxicated on its genius,
And, mad now as it once was,
Crying to God, in its crazed agony:
"O man like myself, O master, I curse you!"

And the least foolish, bold lovers of Madness,
Fleeing the large flock impounded by Destiny,
And taking refuge in the immensity of opium
—Such is the eternal record of the entire globe."

VII

It is bitter knowledge one derives from travel!
The world, monotonous and small, today,
Yesterday, tomorrow, always, shows us our own image:
An oasis of horror in a desert of boredom!

Should we leave? or stay? If you can stay, stay;
Leave, if you must. One man runs, and the next hides
To trick the vigilant fatal enemy,
Time! There are, alas, continual runners,

Like the wandering Jew and like the apostles,
To whom nothing suffices, neither train nor ship,
In order to flee the infamous retiary; there are others
Who can kill him without leaving their cradle.

When at last he puts his foot on our neck,
We can hope and shout: Forward!
As once we left for China,
Our eyes fixed seaward and our hair in the wind,

We shall embark on the sea of darkness
With the joyous heart of a young passenger.
Do you hear those voices, charming and funereal,
Singing: "Come this way, you who wish to eat

The perfumed Lotus! this is where men harvest
The miraculous fruits your heart hungers for;
Come and intoxicate yourself on the strange sweetness
Of that afternoon which never ends"?

By his familiar accent we sense the ghost;
Our Pylades over there extend their arms to us.
"To refresh your courage, swim toward your Electra!"
Says the girl whose knees we once kissed.

VIII

O Death, old captain, the time has come! Let us weigh
    anchor!
This land bores us, O Death! Let us set sail!
If the sky and the sea are as black as ink,
Our hearts which you know are filled with rays!

Pour your poison so that it will comfort us!
The fire searing our brain is such that we want
To plunge to the bottom of the abyss, whether it be
    Heaven or Hell,
To the bottom of the Unknown in order to find some-
    thing *new!*

LESBOS

Mother of Roman games and Greek pleasures,
Lesbos, where kisses, languid or joyous,
Warm as the sun, cool as watermelons,
Are the ornament of nights and glorious days;
Mother of Roman games and Greek pleasures,

Lesbos, where kisses are like cascades
Which fall fearlessly into bottomless gulfs,
And hasten, sobbing and slipping by jerks,
Stormy and secretive, swarming and deep;
Lesbos, where kisses are like cascades!

Lesbos, where Phrynes attract one another,
Where a sigh never remained without an echo,
On a par with Paphos the stars admire you,
And Venus can rightfully be jealous of Sappho!
Lesbos, where Phrynes attract one another,

Lesbos, land of warm and languorous nights,
Which force, O sterile ardor, before their mirrors,
Girls with hollow eyes and amorous bodies
To caress the ripe fruits of their puberty;
Lesbos, land of warm and languorous nights,

Let the severe eyes of old Plato frown;
You exact your pardon from the excess of kisses,
Queen of the sweet empire, loving and noble land,
And of the always inexhaustible subtleties.
Let the severe eyes of old Plato frown.

You exact your pardon from the eternal pain,
Inflicted without respite on ambitious hearts,
Attracted far from us by the radiant smile
Vaguely perceived at the edge of other skies!
You exact your pardon from the eternal pain!

Lesbos, which of the gods will dare be your judge
And condemn your brow grown pale by your work,
If his golden scales have not weighed the deluge
Of tears which your weeping has poured into the sea?
Lesbos, which of the gods will dare be your judge?

What do the laws of the just and the unjust demand
    of us?
Virgins with noble hearts, honor of the isles,
Your religion like others is solemn,
And love will laugh at Hell and Heaven!
What do the laws of the just and the unjust demand
    of us?

For Lesbos has chosen me among all men of the earth
To sing the secret of its flowering virgins,
And as a child I was admitted to the dark mystery
Of frantic laughter mingled with somber tears;
For Lesbos has chosen me among all men of the earth.

From then on I have watched at the top of Leucate,
Like a sentinel with a piercing and accurate eye,
Who watches day and night for brig, tartan or frigate,
Whose distant shapes quiver in the blue;
From then on I have watched at the top of Leucate,

To know whether the sea is indulgent and kind,
And in the sobs with which the rock resounds
One evening will bring back to Lesbos, which forgives,
The worshiped body of Sappho, who left,
To know whether the sea is indulgent and kind!

Of mannish Sappho, lover and poet
More beautiful than Venus in her sad pallor!
—The blue eye is vanquished by the black eye spotted
By the dark circle traced by the suffering
Of mannish Sappho, lover and poet!

—More beautiful than Venus rising over the world
And pouring forth the abundance of her calm
And the radiance of her blond youthfulness
Over the old Ocean delighted with his daughter;
More beautiful than Venus rising over the world!

—Of Sappho who died on the day of her blasphemy,
When, insulting the rite and the designated worship,
She made her beautiful body the supreme prey
Of a brute whose pride punished the impiety
Of the one who died on the day of her blasphemy.

And it is since that time that Lesbos laments,
And, despite the honors which the world pays it,
Exalts every night with the cry of the torment
Which its deserted banks raise toward heaven!
And it is since that time that Lesbos laments!

THE FOUNTAIN

Your beautiful eyes are tired, beloved!
Stay for a long time, without opening them,
In that relaxed pose
Where pleasure left you.
In the courtyard the chattering fountain
Which does not stop night or day,
Sweetly sustains the ecstasy
Into which love this evening plunged me.

> The sheaf opening
> > Into a thousand flowers,
> Where the joyous moon
> > Places its colors,
> Falls like a rain
> > Of heavy tears.

Thus your soul enflamed
By the burning light of pleasure
Rushes, swift and bold,
Toward the vast enchanted skies.
Then, it spills forth, dying,
In a wave of sad languor,
Which along an invisible slope
Descends to the bottom of my heart.

> The sheaf opening
> > Into a thousand flowers,
> Where the joyous moon
> > Places its colors,
> Falls like a rain
> > Of heavy tears.

Beloved, whom the night makes beautiful,
How I love, as I bend over your heart,
To listen to the eternal lament
Which sobs in the fountains!
Moon, sonorous water, blessed night,
Trees trembling nearby,
Your pure melancholy
Is the mirror of my love.

The sheaf opening
　　　Into a thousand flowers,
Where the joyous moon
　　　Places its colors,
Falls like a rain
　　　Of heavy tears.

TO A MALABAR GIRL

Your feet are as refined as your hands, and your hip
Is wide enough to cause envy in the whitest hip;
To the pensive artist your body is sweet and dear;
Your large velvet eyes are blacker than your skin.
In the warm blue country where God had you born,
Your duty is to light the pipe of your master.

To provide the flasks of cold water and perfumes,
To keep far from the bed all curious mosquitoes,
And, as soon as the morning brings a song to the plane
　　　trees,
To buy pineapples and bananas at the bazaar.
All day, wherever you wish, you walk with bare feet,
And softly hum old unknown melodies;
And when evening in its scarlet mantle falls,
You gently stretch your body on a mat,
Where your floating dreams are full of hummingbirds,
And always, like yourself, peaceful and flowering.

Why, happy child, do you want to see our France,
An overpopulated country which suffering mows down,
And, entrusting your life to the strong arms of sailors,
Say grand farewells to your beloved tamarinds?
Half-clothed as you are, with thin muslin,
Shivering in France under snow and hail,
How you would weep for your sweet carefree leisure,
If, with a brutal corset imprisoning your flanks,
You had to glean your supper in our mud
And sell the perfume of your strange charms,
Your eyes pensive, and watching, in our filthy fog,
The scattered phantoms of absent cocoa palms!

EPIGRAPH FOR A CONDEMNED BOOK

Peaceful bucolic reader,
Sober naïve man of good will,
Throw away this saturnine
Orgiastic and melancholy book.

Unless you have studied your rhetoric
With Satan, that wily dean,
Throw it away! You would not understand it,
Or you would believe me hysterical.

But if, without allowing them to be spellbound,
Your eyes can see into abysses,
Read me, in order to learn to love me;

Curious soul who suffer
And are looking for your paradise,
Pity me! . . . Otherwise, I curse you!

MEDITATION

Behave, O my Grief, and keep still.
You asked for Evening; it is descending; here it is:
A dark atmosphere covers the city,
Bearing peace to some, and worry to others.

While the wretched crowd of mortals,
Under the whip of Pleasure, that merciless torturer,
Goes to collect remorse in the servile festivity,
My Grief, give me your hand; come this way,

Far off from them. See the Years that have died leaning
Over the balconies of heaven, in old-fashioned dresses;
See my Regret in smiles rising up from the depths of
      the water;

The dying Sun going to sleep under an arch,
And, like a long shroud dragging toward the East,
Hear, my beloved, hear the steps of sweet night.

THE ABYSS

Pascal had his abyss, which moved with him.
Alas! everything is an abyss—action, desire, dreams,
Words! and over my hair which stands upright
I often feel the wind of Fear pass.

Above and below, everywhere, distances, shores,
Silence, terrifying imprisoning space . . .
Over the depths of my nights God with His knowing
    finger
Draws a multiform traceless nightmare.

I fear sleep as one fears a great hole,
Full of vague horror, leading one knows not where;
I see only infinity through all my windows,

And my mind, always haunted by vertigo,
Is jealous of the insensibility of the void.
—Ah! I will never be free of Numbers and Beings!

COMPLAINTS OF AN ICARUS

The lovers of prostitutes
Are happy, free and satisfied;
As for me, my arms are broken
Over embracing clouds.

Thanks to the extraordinary stars,
Which shine in the depths of the sky,
My consumed eyes see only
Memories of suns.

In vain I tried to find
The end of space and its middle;
Under some fiery eye or other
I feel my wing breaking;

And burned by love of beauty,
I will not have the sublime honor
Of giving my name to the abyss
Which will serve me as a tomb.

Notes

Page 16: The Latin title is the opening of Psalm 130: "Out of the depths have I cried unto thee."

Duellum is the archaic form of bellum (war), with a special connotation of two participants.

Page 18: The Latin title Semper Eadem ("always the same") is either a feminine singular or a neuter plural.

Page 24: The Latin title means "The sorrowful, wandering woman."

Page 26: Baudelaire probably found the (Greek) title ("The Self-Torturer") in Joseph de Maistre ("3e Entretien" of the Soirées de Saint-Pétersbourg); it is the title of a Latin play by Terence based on an earlier Greek play.

Alphabetical List of Titles

Alphabetical List of First Lines

53

DOVER·THRIFT·EDITIONS

All books complete and unabridged. All 5³⁄₁₆″ × 8¹⁄₄″, paperbound.
Just $1.00–$2.00 in U.S.A.

A selection of the more than 100 titles in the series:

FLATLAND: A ROMANCE OF MANY DIMENSIONS, Edwin A. Abbott. 96pp. 27263-X $1.00

DOVER BEACH AND OTHER POEMS, Matthew Arnold. 112pp. 28037-3 $1.00

CIVIL WAR STORIES, Ambrose Bierce. 128pp. 28038-1 $1.00

THE DEVIL'S DICTIONARY, Ambrose Bierce. 144pp. 27542-6 $1.00

SONGS OF INNOCENCE AND SONGS OF EXPERIENCE, William Blake. 64pp. 27051-3 $1.00

SONNETS FROM THE PORTUGUESE AND OTHER POEMS, Elizabeth Barrett Browning. 64pp. 27052-1 $1.00

MY LAST DUCHESS AND OTHER POEMS, Robert Browning. 128pp. 27783-6 $1.00

SELECTED POEMS, George Gordon, Lord Byron. 112pp. 27784-4 $1.00

ALICE'S ADVENTURES IN WONDERLAND, Lewis Carroll. 96pp. 27543-4 $1.00

O PIONEERS!, Willa Cather. 128pp. 27785-2 $1.00

THE CHERRY ORCHARD, Anton Chekhov. 64pp. 26682-6 $1.00

THE AWAKENING, Kate Chopin. 128pp. 27786-0 $1.00

THE RIME OF THE ANCIENT MARINER AND OTHER POEMS, Samuel Taylor Coleridge. 80pp. 27266-4 $1.00

HEART OF DARKNESS, Joseph Conrad. 80pp. 26464-5 $1.00

THE RED BADGE OF COURAGE, Stephen Crane. 112pp. 26465-3 $1.00

A CHRISTMAS CAROL, Charles Dickens. 80pp. 26865-9 $1.00

THE CRICKET ON THE HEARTH AND OTHER CHRISTMAS STORIES, Charles Dickens. 128pp. 28039-X $1.00

SELECTED POEMS, Emily Dickinson. 64pp. 26466-1 $1.00

SELECTED POEMS, John Donne. 96pp. 27788-7 $1.00

NOTES FROM THE UNDERGROUND, Fyodor Dostoyevsky. 96pp. 27053-X $1.00

SIX GREAT SHERLOCK HOLMES STORIES, Sir Arthur Conan Doyle. 112pp. 27055-6 $1.00

THE SOULS OF BLACK FOLK, W. E. B. Du Bois. 176pp. 28041-1 $2.00

MEDEA, Euripides. 64pp. 27548-5 $1.00

A BOY'S WILL AND NORTH OF BOSTON, Robert Frost. 112pp. (Available in U.S. only) 26866-7 $1.00

WHERE ANGELS FEAR TO TREAD, E. M. Forster. 128pp. (Available in U.S. only) 27791-7 $1.00

FAUST, PART ONE, Johann Wolfgang von Goethe. 192pp. 28046-2 $2.00

THE SCARLET LETTER, Nathaniel Hawthorne. 192pp. 28048-9 $2.00

A DOLL'S HOUSE, Henrik Ibsen. 80pp. 27062-9 $1.00

THE TURN OF THE SCREW, Henry James. 96pp. 26684-2 $1.00

VOLPONE, Ben Jonson. 112pp. 28049-7 $1.00

DUBLINERS, James Joyce. 160pp. 26870-5 $1.00

A PORTRAIT OF THE ARTIST AS A YOUNG MAN, James Joyce. 192pp. 28050-0 $2.00

LYRIC POEMS, John Keats. 80pp. 26871-3 $1.00

THE BOOK OF PSALMS, King James Bible. 144pp. 27541-8 $1.00